Mostly the Wind

Mostly the Wind
John Peter Harn

Flowstone Press

Mostly the Wind
Copyright 2022 © John Peter Harn

Cover Image by Emily Clugston
Author Photo by Jessica Harn
All images used with permission

First Flowstone Press Edition • May 2022
ISBN 978-1-945824-53-1

Flowstone Press,
an Imprint of Left Fork
www.leftforkbooks.com

It wasn't easy, waking up wise,
knowing too much about the moon.
It was hard to accept that my grandfather's face,
occulted in his old diamond ring, was on my finger now
and that all this ubiquitous ivy, overgrowing everything,
somehow traced back to me.
But work was work and I needed a job
so I made two rules to help me
climb the mountain I perceived…
   - Say it in a whisper.
   - Find it in the wind.

Table of Contents

I	I'm asking	5
	Lifting the Veil	6
	A leaf-blower ruined	7
	Drinking coffee in plain air	8
	Sunbathing on a park bench	9
	Morning Walk	10
	The point about wind	11
	Hendricks Park	12
	A ten-year-old boy	13
	your life is saved	14
II	Commonplace Event	19
	Office	20
	Girlfriend	21
	Amanda's Three Virtues	22
	My neighbor the recluse and I	23
	Flight to Albuquerque	24
	Salvation Army Finds $5,000 Diamond Ring in Donation Kettle	25
	An American in Rome	26
	None of the Toil	27
	He meets an old friend for beers	28
	Meeting for coffee	29
	Hiking the Trail at Sweet Creek Falls	30
III	Q&A Between Two Stoned Friends Sitting on a Sunlit Log	35
	Patriot's Dream	36
	How to Pay for Napalm	37
	Born With It	38
	Nostalgic for Now	39
	Hushed Leaves, Nixon and Despair	40
	Yes, I kept your high school graduation picture	41
	Ordinary Day	42

IV	To be Of a Place and Not Just From	47
	Lesser-known Deities	48
	Art's not	52
	He knows	53
	Opposites	54
	Obit	58
V	Memory for Abe	63
	Why You Left Italy for America at Fourteen	64
	Family History	66
	Eugene, Oregon, 1980, The Year You were Born	67
	Hunting the Elusive Columbia Gorge Salamander	68
	Better Things to Do	70
	Visiting my Great-Aunt's Grave, Kenesaw Nebraska	71
	In Dayton Ohio, in 1919,	74
	Death in the Age of Facebook	76
	Planks It Borrowed from the Wind	77

Acknowledgements	79
Notes	80
About the Author	82

Mostly the Wind

I

*I have a feeling that my boat has struck,
down there in the depths, against a great thing.
And nothing happens! Nothing...Silence...Waves...
Or has everything happened,
and are we standing now in the new life?*

- Juan Ramon Jimenez -

I'm asking

what I've always asked for:

to sit under a molten sun
on the doorstep of the abyss
peer in and never recover.

Tanning on a patch of grass
I've learned a lot this summer:

drink extra water in July
synchronize with the fireflies
find common cause with the ants.

A squadron of florescent bees
takes a sudden interest in me.
They fan out, scan me in the infrared
square me with pi, fly off.

With the right head tilt
even heavy traffic can
sound like a river.

Lifting the Veil

It's a little like the time
that old cotton dress of yours
stiff and dry on a clothesline
got a taste of self-awareness in a downpour

or that time, stopped at a traffic light
you realized all the bone in you
had a secret pact with stone

and it's a lot like that time
you were having a glass of wine on the Strand
and the evening sun, setting over the tranquil bay
grabbed you by the collar and pulled you in

because in the rush
of everything to become
something else
once in a great while
the curtain goes up.

A leaf-blower ruined

the silence that was mentoring me.

I was minding my own business
sitting on a park bench
suspending belief
getting rid of up and down
growing eyes in the back of my head
when a leaf-blower shut me down
and yanked me back ruined
from where I was to here.

Maybe we need some new laws
to protect what's left of the habitat of saints:

   Sitting cross-legged, inheriting.
     - holding its own for now -

   Watching crane flies gather at dusk.
     - they're the last of their kind -

   Tying a daisy-chain around a six-year-old's wrist.
     - already lost so never mind -

Somewhere on the eroded flats of the Great American West
a man watches the sun set from the roof of his car.
Alone in a jurisdiction of one,
he burns sweetgrass in a terracotta pot.

Drinking coffee in plain air

in a road-side desert town
waiting for night.

Morning passes.
Noon never comes, but evening does
beamed from the cell phones of tourists
who fall out of air-conditioned vans
buy snacks and drive away.

I've come to find the words
to bear these dunes alone
to doze-off if I can
and wake at the hub of harmonic
embedded in amber.

At midnight the sky tastes like peppermint.
A crescent moon cradles the liquid eye of Jupiter.

All along the razor's edge
almond light erupts.

Sunbathing on a park bench

in the peak burning hours
the sun begins to recycle me.

Two women jog by
on their way to the rendezvous
where the ripple began
to disassemble themselves
back into pieces of the perpetuity.

Eyes closed, I hear the whoosh
of air in their lungs
the grab and release
of their shoes on the tarmac.

They have a head start
but they'll find me there when they arrive
on my hands and knees
almost transparent
pawing through a pile of shell and bone.

Morning Walk

I planned to get some work done today
after a walk through the park
but when I sat down to rest
in the shade halfway through
a finch joined me
and when our eyes locked
I slipped into uselessness.

Maybe my name will go first
unpronounced, crossing the gap
from irrelevant to forgotten.
And maybe this spark I've carried and spent
will follow my name
slowly dimming in an updraft
pulling a scrap of hair
and hide behind it on a tether.

If I leaned in, just a little
and laughed under my breath.
If I made the sign of the cross…

The point about wind

is it makes you run fast.

Twenty first graders fly into recess
finding ways to run.
They squeal if they get tagged
and bolt off twice as fast.
They weave the gauntlet of pendulum swings
or dash the length of a chain-link fence
strumming it like a giant's guitar.

When the whistle blows to go inside
they don't hear it at first
above the din of their alliances.
When they jam the single door, it's
two-steps-forward, one-step-back
a bottleneck made
accidentally on purpose.

Back in their seats, they flap their wings to cool off.
The teacher allows as long as it takes
for their hearts to slow down.
She strolls the aisles, modeling calm
touches the top of each child's head
says each name out loud
and in return each child says *here*.

The point about sun
is how it feels against your skin.

The point about wind
is it makes you run fast.

Hendricks Park

She doesn't know he saw her
toss an acorn to a jay
saw the kindness she channeled like a river
and the respect that made her arm
move with no threat
and the trust that lets the jay
loop to the lowest branch
with an acorn in its mouth.

A small stream passes nearby
translating instructions on what to keep.
Hummingbirds and finches take turns
bathing in it, washing wildfire feathers
in sweetened blue air.

So when, after spending some time like this
alone together, draped in white silence
their invitation arrives
to take up residency in the far-flung empire
of those who cross-over and don't come back
of course they accept.
Leave their things on the bench.
Step into light.

A ten-year-old boy

finds a fossil in a stream
and tries to keep it
to the end of his forever
in a pouch, a box, a drawer, a house
but it gets away from him
somewhere in his thirties
and stays lost for decades
only to turn up
in the stream of his things in the end
in the outflow of what he collected
the garnets, abalone, glass and fool's gold
the agates, amber and bone
all of it tumbling in a downstream flow
of memory and dream
falling out as the current broadens and slows
heavy things first, then the light
until the fossil ends up
somewhere brand new
covered with silt and lost in new time
as if it hadn't passed
through the hands of a heartbeat
explorer.

your life is saved

if you have coos unspent
from when you were cuddled and small

if someone brushed your hair before school
and was happy when you came home

if kisses were blown
from your doorway at night
kisses you plucked from the air and swallowed

if an amber light lit your hall

if your window framed a tree

if you knew the names of a couple bright stars

II

*We are like butterflies who flutter for a day
and think it is forever.*

- Carl Sagan -

Commonplace Event

A man behind the wheel
of a shiny new sedan
first in line at a busy intersection
is bored with his commute
and reaches over the passenger seat
for the cord on the floor
that he needs to open his playlist
when his foot skates off
the brake too soon
and stomps the panic gas instead
turning a woman in the crosswalk
into blinding light
erupting through a pinhole
and a rush of flapping wings.

Office

Yes, he's at work today
phone charged and fingertipped
but he won't answer it.
Cast-off shoes in the desk well
are tickets to somewhere.
He forwards his emails
to random people. Rain again
and a soaked parking lot.
Outside his second story window
his car is third from left.
Once he was a part
of the voices down the hall.
He kept everyone's plants alive
the receptionist laughing.
He had good cause:
kids and nervous in-laws. Now
it's bills and an abandoned dog.
True, his money still quadruples
his boss's, but that's far too sheer
a ribbon to hold on to.
He's always been free
to quit anytime
ricocheting became irresistible.
Today he's remembering it.
At his computer he types
How far can the soul wander
before the body demands equal time?
and deletes it.
He stands at the window
ankle-deep in forever.
Cars hiss on the wet street.
A girl walks across the parking lot.

Girlfriend
for Carol

They're driving up for the weekend
your son and his new girlfriend
because it's time you met this
girl of superlatives
and because you'll absolutely love her.
So you set the patio table for tea
trying to remember how it feels
to have your heart hacked.
Tires crunch and you peek through an old lace curtain.
She steps out of the car in a chocolate body leotard
strawberry apron and wingtip sunglasses
and you admit, yes, she does
look a bit fantastic, like she cuts
rubies or teaches
fencing for a living.
They stretch their legs in your driveway
tease out the last secret giggle
and walk up to your door.
He to whom you passed the spark
and she who holds it for safekeeping.
Pleasantries and a woman's hinged handshake.
The welcome sweep of your smile-shaped arm.
Over tea she says, *See that jar of nuts*
and bolts on your windowsill over there?
It's as important as anything else
if you stop and think about it.
You smile and keep quiet.
It's his turn now, to catch the flaming baton.
The floral tablecloth seduces your spoon.
You *are* going to love this girl.

Amanda's Three Virtues

Amanda writes a two-page letter in cursive to her grandpa.
At the post office, dimes and pennies in her hand, she puts
the stamp on by herself. She pictures him when he opens it,
smiling, leaning against the fridge. On her way out, in the sun-
streaked lobby, near the double glass doors: Prosperity. She
hums on the way home, a soft back-up to the cosmos' soft lead.
When she rounds the last corner
the tree in her yard turns white.

Amanda spoons fresh peaches on her nine-year-old's pancakes.
She sweeps the day clean for a road trip. They make a beeline
for nowhere. She says yes when he wants to pull over, pile out,
run breakneck through radiant corn. She lets him spin off, to
be alone with green. She doesn't answer when he calls. He goes
quiet too. She's glad he's discovering kernels and silk
handling fat leaves
peeling back a place they almost blew by.

Amanda drives out of town in her old convertible, pulled by
the rays of a god-sent sunset. She follows the centerline until
it runs out, tire-tracks into dirt, stubble-fields into midnight.
Stopped at an overlook, top down, in a rusty spur of the
mighty Milky Way, she puts her seat back
and laces her fingers behind her head.
Crickets. Star-sweep.
The distant beam of a headland lighthouse.

My neighbor the recluse and I

bump into each other at midnight in the alley
on our way to the dumpster
carrying bags of trash.

Nice night, I say.
Yeah, he says, trailing off   looking up
at a sky full of stars. He sighs.
It's everywhere, man,   he says.
You know what I'm talkin' about.
Guys like us.   Old fucks.   It's on us now.
Haul it up like a whale.
Drag it around like a fuckin' anchor.
You know what I'm talkin' about.
I see you walkin' around town.
Guys like us.   We look up
and we stay there man,   we stay there,   he says,
pointing straight up
looking straight at me
the words in his mouth like iron flowers.

I let the dumpster lid slam
a little too hard, brush off my hands
and look him in the eye
trying to remember his name.
He sees me searching for words,
smiles and falls quiet.

In moonlight, at the dumpster,
bare-chested in pajama bottoms,
my neighbor the recluse
wants me to say we are gods.

Flight to Albuquerque

She buckles her seatbelt, vowing never to work stupid again.
She's heard good things about Albuquerque, its master plan, its
Pueblo ramparts, its armistice with the sun. When the seatbelt
light goes off, the six-year-old boy next to her, someone else's
child, lowers his tray-table to share his coloring book and
bag of markers. He opens to a clean page and presses it flat.
His father shuts his eyes against the window, wide-awake
and listening. They start at the corners and work toward
the middle. Purple is their hands-down favorite. Green is
number two. Her life in LA was so pedestrian. She felt like an
architect doodling garages. Or a bird in the rafters of a home-
improvement store. But today she's naming colors for the first
time. Naming while coloring, while trading, naming while
deciding, rolling the vowels in her mouth like sugared air. She
wonders how high the curbs are in Albuquerque, how wide
the sidewalks, what the tree-code provides regarding shading.
She imagines herself running to greet the boy's mother, outside
baggage, grasping her elbows and kissing her cheeks like a
seasoned Continental. The flight passes quickly. Dusk defines
their descent. They stow their work, return their tray-tables
to their original, upright position. Deep in the golden hour,
Albuquerque, the open city, the luminous map, rises up like a
puffed sweetbread. She leans in for a better view.
Looks promising, she says to her new friend.
Like a bowl of multi-colored yarn.
Like a blanket not asking permission to become.

*Salvation Army Finds $5,000 Diamond Ring
 in Donation Kettle*
                            -Tacoma Tribune

I think the ringing bell steeled her
and cracked her defenses
as she stood to one side
wondering how much to give.

She said she did it
because the Salvation Army hired her father
at the last minute during the Depression
after his own father traded the icebox
for more bread than they could eat
then disappeared
because there wasn't enough
reason not to
jump from a soup line into a well.

His mother took in boarders, laundry, anything,
but nothing worked except the son
mending clothes for an army of poor,
for a paycheck that launched him
into the acid spray of war
across decades of factory floors, marriage, kids
all the way to the smooth obsidian edge
where he teetered for a second
before taking the swan-dive plunge
he'd practiced all his life.

At least, that's why she *said* she did it.
But I think gravity helped her
wedding ring fall
and I bet she walked away
ten pounds lighter, in a milky-white light
wearing her first buddha smile.

An American in Rome

His wife goes shopping
while he waits for her in a Renaissance church
sitting in pew with his heart in his hand.

He sees the old ones
pressing forward in tunics and leggings
ordinary folk, broken by mass
crowding the altar for a glimpse of the masterpiece
hungry for scraps of bread and immortality.

*How true it must have been, how bedrock
the saints' passion and the artists' genius
clasping hands across time, under the tutelage of Jesus himself.
But where is their truth now? Did they leave it here for safekeeping?
And is that why I sit in here chains?
Or is it gone, and is this church more
a finger pointing to than a place possessed?*

On one hand, two acolytes kneel
at an alcove altar, in abject humility.
On the other, the ambient
blue glow of their phones.

None of the Toil

He got used to believing
he hadn't wasted his life
when a letter arrived that made those rafters shift.

He remembers the tree-lined road she remembers
and the red clay dust on their bare feet
and the honeysuckle she says overgrew them.
But none of the toil she recalls
comes back to him now
the climbing out of ditches and the falling back in.

His mind sticks instead
on the view from Pyramid Point
when she, in cut-offs, skipped stones across
that summer they lived at Higgins Lake.

Her letter reminds him why
when he combs the beach these days
he only hunts a certain kind of shell
the calla lily spiral, polished to a twist
plunging and flaring at the same time
because hidden inside them
assumed but out of view
burn flecks of fool's gold.

He meets an old friend for beers

and hand feeds their camaraderie
pretzels, in case bottle-clinks
and bandaged references to a girl
don't carry them
all the way to closing
when something new unfurls
inside his beer, a mist
psychoactive if inhaled
inhaled.

Back home, alone, head a bag of stars
he unearths photos of his first steady girl
from a box in his closet
stunned by how beautiful she is
allowed to be now
that he's finally stripped
the last thing from the last thing
having pulled forty years-worth
of shingles off by hand.

He imagines which fields she walked
what names she gave to whom
from where she watched her vantage points change.

Sitting cross-legged on his bedroom floor
he hears her laugh
but just the memory of it
would've been enough.

Meeting for coffee

after thirty-odd years,
memories fly like moths from a jar.

Their first kiss in the beer garden. How long it took to land. How it poured once it started, like whiskey into wine. And their last kiss too, after how many years? Against a parked car. A murmuration of kisses. A shape-shifting swarm in the cage of their mouths, until it saw blue sky and flew.

Deep breaths in the glare of so much remembering.
White space.

She asks him if he thinks a trap ensnares
people who live in the past
if that adage handed down by sages from on high
might be true.

His *no* rolls across the table and teeters on the edge.
She catches it when it falls.

And as the filament they each
hold one end of starts to glow
they wonder, in shape and color more than words
what if they whistled
to attract it, left a light on, a door ajar
if they snagged it by the wrist when it passed in the dark
like a rescued child.

If he stroked her cheek with the back of his hand.
If she closed her eyes.
If they found their old pulse
still beating in some distant sleep.

Hiking the Trail at Sweet Creek Falls

It's their very first time
on this rooty-wet trail, built, the sign says
by volunteer lovers of Oregon's tumbling firs.
Every ten yards they stop to soak up
some pious new green. Dew makes it personal.
And when moss-draped walls or the hulks of old growth
narrow the trail, making them walk single file
she in front and he in back, her voice gets lost
in hurried water and he can't catch what she's saying
but he follows her timbre and pitch
and the intonation she's stitched to their step-by-step
well enough to guess
she's recounting conversations with friends.
And when they stop to catch their breath
at a wide spot on the trail, face-to-face
with falling water, and she asks him what he meant
by *misanthrope* in the car
when he used it to describe his way
of mapping the world, he's impressed she isn't content
to let it go, a word without much lift
in the soil she's rooted in.
So he answers obliquely, the hardest kind
of reply to get right, to show respect
saying these falls don't sense them passing through
that they'll be here long after they've given up
warm beds, hot teas and dreams of eclairs.
And when he says they might
side-step what confounds them
if they hold that thought for long in their heads
and *that's*, more or less, what he meant in the car
she takes his hand, warms it in hers, blows on it
and folds them into the chatter of Sweet Creek Falls.

III

Under each station of the real, another glimmers.

- Marcel Proust -

Q&A Between Two Stoned Friends Sitting on a Sunlit Log

Friend 1:
So. If any music anywhere
is, like you say
crap to someone somewhere
and sublime to someone else

and if there is an upright piano somewhere
as you say, in upstate New York
ignored for decades
and bearing its water rings alone

and if there's an old steel drum
like you also say
somewhere in the shade of a Caribbean palm
stuck in sand and pocked by salt air

couldn't one argue, by extension,
that *every* pulsed wave is
crap and sublime
and neither can cancel the other one out?

Friend 2 grins
and points with his thumb to a bumble bee
a few feet away
loaded with pollen
tethered to its pivots
deaf dumb and blind.

Patriot's Dream

I'm dreaming of a country
where handshakes are stirred more than shaken
and finger-foods cuddle
mildly alcoholic desserts.
Where, at the border, an Elvis impersonator
stamps the back of your hand with a happy face
and waves you in.
Where clothes change hue to match skin tone
of which there is infinite variety
and toddlers ride their parents' shoulders
drunk on chocolate milk and French fries.
I'm dreaming of a country where Jesus is rendered in wax
and displayed at the visitor's center, next to Piltdown Man
each with an informative placard.
I'm dreaming of a country where everyone is a tourist
flush with cash and invested in land.
Where sidewalk musicians play the songs they know
and couples hear the songs they love.
Where the dead wink and whisper
guarantees to the living
and a hint of lemon-mint hangs above the reservoir.
I'm dreaming of a country where lovers still stroll
down meandering sidewalks at twilight
and gather at the village green
to hear a banjo pluck its way through the pathos
of fireworks painting
waves and waves of amber grain.

How to Pay for Napalm

Streetlights.
The Sunday funnies.
Warm towels from the dryer.
Bifocals on a TV Guide.
Two-for-one footwear, through Sunday.
A touch-tone phone, wall-mount, beige.
Iced tea on a coaster.
A box fan in a window.
Matching pillows in the guest room.
Rabbit ears. Frosting in a can.
Five dollars in a birthday card.
A yellow porchlight.
A screen door on a spring.
A high school scoreboard.
A corsage in the fridge. Cufflinks in a drawer.
Magazines on a coffee table.
A hosed-off lawnmower on an asphalt drive.
A bright white mailbox with a little red flag.
Small talk with Mrs. Cook
standing in line for the next available teller.

Born With It

No one *makes* you feel the weight
added to your bus's tires
every time a passenger climbs aboard.

That's just you.

Likewise, no one *makes* you choose
between the driver, observing his gauges
or the woman's labored breathing behind you.

These are entirely your own investments.

And last week, too
having tea with your neighbor
no one *made* you fixate
on the potted plant behind her
every time she spoke, a pale, floppy aloe
years too big for its container.

Nothing she said could deflect its broadcast.

These are your talents
acquired in the womb
when your mother's heartbeat paced yours:

Hearing rogue waves, far off.

Knowing what comes after *equals*.

Feeling how thin the incarnate is.

Nostalgic for Now

She's still around, living on the island
taking it easy, waiting for nothing
much as usual.
But she finds herself missing things lately
she hasn't lost yet
and pining for things she still has
like pelicans
plying shorelines, above it all
big enough to tip the tilt
and blankets of oleander
petals underfoot
downed by wind and matted by rain.
And she's starting to miss
herself somehow too
in the midst of all her seeing
to wax nostalgic for the flame she still has
in the palm of her hand
cupped against wind
still warm, still flickering
but now somehow inexplicably mourned.

Hushed Leaves, Nixon and Despair
for Deborah

High school, junior year, fall of '71,
up to our knees in Nixon and despair
for weeks we skipped fourth period
to get high after lunch
in the ravine behind the scoreboard.

Who could blame us for wanting peace and quiet
in the rambling death-throes of the 60s,
wanting hushed leaves and small words
in a secluded space, where branches brushed the dome,
meaning nothing, and we could be suspended
in thin air for a while.

I still keep a matchbook from those days
on which you wrote, in blue ink:
> *Here lies our beautiful erasure.*
> *Raccoons will guide us from now on.*
> *All is well.*

Sometimes, when the weather is fine
and there's nothing much to do
a memory of you asks to be revised.

I refuse,
then comply.

Yes, I kept your high school graduation picture

in my wallet forty years
a relic of the days before
money hammered us into tools.

But I took it out
every now and then, maybe once a year
to kill time waiting
in a restaurant for example
to show my girls and wonder out loud
if a gale had blown that day in '78
grounding the ferry I took
from you to here
what kind of life that storm
might've offered us instead.

Your passing reminded me
waves exist
inside vibrations
the peaks and valleys what we call song.

Ordinary Day

There have been other days like this one.
Same temp, humidity, sunrise and sunset
same low blooms and high clouds

but none with this heart, exactly
or this cognitive tilt, or these helium prayers
and none with these exact gleams
in these exact eyes.

So who can really say
much about today
if no one knows and no one's yet counted
which waves broke which shores
what held fast, what let go,
and who set out to start again where.

IV

You have to dive down, as it were, and sink more rapidly than that which sinks in advance of you.

- Franz Kafka -

To be Of a Place and Not Just From

Banana-seat bikes
outside a cinderblock market -
two boys in line with quarters.

A hidden footpath
in a field of tall grass -
generations of cats at the same feeding bowl.

A distant train
whistle at night -
the calling card of everywhere else.

Lesser-known Deities

*

The God of Old Cemeteries
wants a change of venue after fifty years at St. John's. Still, she keeps up appearances. Brushed-back hair and a nice cotton dress. When visitors come in broad daylight, she's all, *Sorry about the weeds,* and, *I've been meaning to fix that gate.* But when couples show up on hot summer nights, for dark skies and cool grass, she acts like she's not home. She doesn't run them off. She knows how much headstones need and how little they ask. At dawn, muffled voices, car doors, tires creeping down the long gravel drive.

A tea kettle whistles in the caretaker's cottage
where she sleeps in case things go wrong
but they never do.

*

The God of Free Association
has an ad in the *Weekly Shopper.* His preschool needs a teacher.
The God of Old Cemeteries drops by for a chat. No credential,
no experience, but he likes the ellipses she puts at the front
of her sentences. They sip pastel tea from little white cups.
Trying to recruit her, he confides that once, in his teens, he
shot arrows blindly into a canyon, telling his father he'd been
busy with target practice. His father, suspicious, went to check.
Bullseyes had chased the arrows down, he tells her. *Every arrow
found its mark.*

She raises an eyebrow
waiting the perfect interval before answering.
…I see your point, she says. *About the children.*

*

The God of Introspection
sleeps in snow blown up against his cabin door, off highway 47 near mile-marker 12. It takes him forever to sort snowflakes into lineages and drop them in the matrix he designed but can't explain. Forever is something he has plenty of. In spring, when the forest breaks into trees, and the trees break into branches, and the branches break into leaves, he's there too, in sapwood with the burrowers.

He's happy near the bottom rung of things.
He doesn't want to be fished out.
He didn't ask for biscuits and jam.

*

The God of Excess
wakes up in the street at 3am, flat on her back, a few blocks
from her apartment complex. She doesn't know where she is
or if she's hurt. No one is standing around this time, mouthing
words. No ghostly faces painted in phone-glow. No second-
string stretcher crew, elbowing in.

Just the God of Excess,
alone under a flickering streetlight
reaching up with both hands for the belt of Orion.

Art's not

the thing *produced*, he says.
It's not a black and white glossy or a cast-bronze nymph.
Not brushstrokes
herding your eye to a vanishing point
or hips coiled around a gorgeous riff.
It's not the verb you steal when sunlight spills
over the limb of a fingernail moon
or that dome in Rome
floating over the jeweled crypt of a stylized prince.

Exactly! she says.
It's more like the opal that slips
off your finger and falls
end over end down a well.
It's not the *plink* at the bottom
or the echo of it all.
It's the fall… she says,
… the fall,

and rolls him off her
like a swampy log
hooking a lock of his long damp hair
behind his flushed ear.

He knows

what's outside his walls.

He's flown that flag
drunk that wine
been that rich.

But he knows too, the opposite.
The glossy at the center
its acute sensitivity
its shoreline completely unexplored.

So which is it?

Does he, like milkweed
take the wind as a lover
migrate north and south
and find his joy alone?

Or does he enlist
pass the bottle with his mates
uncork the ancient drinking songs
and goosestep off to war?

Opposites

*

The Opposite of Westward Ho
is a tabletop's love for a fine lace doily.

You have your eye on a Conestoga wagon and a team of
mules but a pitcher of lemonade and a leather-bound hymnal
conspire against you. And August's bayed roof. And Nan's
chickens, too many for the coop. You fill a bucket at the well
and carry it inside. Children, some yours, some not, hold
hands at the hearth with their backs to you, singing a song they
learned in school about Paradise.

They don't see you come in.
They don't see you go out.
They don't hear you pleading with the well.

*

The Opposite of Amazing Grace
is a baked potato wrapped in tinfoil.

This summer's been too hot for foot-tapping. Your window screen deflects a bee but the bump passes through, warming your house a little more. Meanwhile, somewhere in the great far-off, out of earshot, a murder of crows escalates over a strip of something red.

Evening arrives on a metronome.
You open the door.
The ticking passes through.

*

The Opposite of a Luau
is a middle-aged woman
carrying groceries over the threshold of her ranch-style home.

The Silverado in her garage has ridiculous knobby tires. The stalagmites in her laundry room are made of paper plates. Jars of peaches on her kitchen shelf reflect the motif of the wallpaper there. After a glass of Chardonnay and some *Wheel of Fortune*, she slips into a restless nap, under a beige and brown afghan she knitted for herself.

In an overstuffed chair, in the spray of her plasma TV
she dreams she's untangling the tiki torches and party lights
the previous owners left in the shed.

*

The Opposite of a Phobia
is stopping for a hitchhiker
with an open jar of gasoline in a blistering July.

Mixed into topsoil in your backyard: Napped flint,
strontium-90, genocidal beads. Everywhere beaches are littered
with the teeth of men who jumped through fire. Wind gusts. A
man looks up, his bloodshot eyes in the grip of premonition.

Cables on the seafloor,
corpses at the poles.
Garbage strewn across the moon.

Obit

He grew up believing
he wasn't born as much as calved
from a limestone outcropping
in a sunbathed somewhere, in Ohio.

He found comfort knowing
no matter where he went or who he was with
a boy with a cowlick stood beside him
researching the breeze, taking notes on a clipboard
with a pencil tied to a string.

Under his bed, Indian corn in a draw-string pouch
fossils in a battered wooden box.

He had a recurring dream in which he followed a trail
of mist to the pool beneath
the falls at Old Man's Cave
where he found a door wedged between two trees
mossy in the spray and hopelessly out of plumb.

It only opened wide enough
for his hand to pass through.

On the other side, his fingers curled and straightened
straightened and curled
testing the air like a moth's proboscis.

V

*I learned how to find the new moon
by looking for the circular absence of stars.*

- Kazim Ali -

Memory for Abe

I wasn't brave enough when I was four
to walk the long dirt drive under braided elms
to play with the boy next door
that summer we lived in Xenia, Ohio.

But I memorized the dance those black leaves made
on that long dirt drive
and the backlit eyes of the amber-headed boy
waiting on his porch with something
bright blue in his hand.

Even at four I knew
that scene would pass like stone into memory.

And now you, grandson, four years old
and very amber yourself
find me in my favorite chair
put a bright blue toy in my hand
and walk away.

Fireflies and heat-lightening
are the other memories of that summer.
Voices through a window screen.
Rhubarb pie.

Why You Left Italy for America at Fourteen
for Romolo

Because no one could say for sure
when they buried your father next to your mother
if he found her there in her wedding dress
like he said he would.

And because his bed sheets flapped
in the wind for a week
before you took them down.

And because you had no strength after that
to climb the forty steps to mass
no matter how hard they rang the bell.

But mostly it was the wind
scouring your hill-top town from a new direction
murmuring in a tongue you couldn't understand
though you knew the intonation
of regret when you heard it.

So you packed a leather case
wool vest and pants, silk scarf and cotton shirt
tucked the only photo of your mother in a secret lining
and left.

Parting sheep with catcalls, Mario took you
by wagon over ice-age roads
to catch the train in Campobasso.

Twenty dollars in your pocket to last a lifetime
you gave him a handful of strawberries for his trouble.

For you, steam whistles, black tunnels, Naples' scalding noon,
weeks in steerage aboard the *Citta di Napoli*.
The spires of New York.

But Mario, in no hurry to get home, stopped at an overlook.
Eyes fixed on infinity
he ate your berries one-by-one
and took your message back to Fossalto.

Family History

Yes, we had weight
and mass, and a coil of rope
on a hook in the garage.

We had firewood stacked
against a fence, a Rambler and a cookout grill
ice skates and a frozen pond.

There was Communion, Easter, Confirmation and Prom
smoldering leaves and tripping roots
a pickaxe, tar paper and bricks
and an attic pull-string
hanging in the hall.

But it was, it turns out,
immaterial, after all,
atom and germ
briefly congealed and quickly dispersed

like after a squall passes
when the wind dies down
when all that's left is the telling
and some branches in the yard.

Eugene, Oregon, 1980, The Year You were Born

It was that summer your mom and I
had all the tomatoes and cornbread we wanted,
when our neighbor brought us our mail
and her collie wagged its tail while we chatted.

It was the summer we built-out the porch
with windows we got at the salvage yard,
when mint and wild carrot trotted off across our tongues
and breezes pushed the field through the trees.

We said we'd never seen
day and night so in sync.
So many berries.
Such porcelain skies.

Hunting the Elusive Columbia Gorge Salamander

You check in on me, every so often
to make sure my feet are still in the creek
and I'm still in the chair where your mother put me
before she melted into the forest
in search of solitude and mushrooms.
I'm to watch you look for salamanders
here in this fir-filled hollow of our late summer
not far from Crown Point.
Wading in rubber boots, you keep your own counsel
on what to lift and how deep to dig
flexing your new-found power
to do no harm. But it occurs to you
I might know some things
about creeks. You heard I was
a boy once too. So when you find a tadpole
unsure of what it is, thrown off
by its flared head, tail-whip and strident leglessness
you bring it to me in tightly cupped hands
to get my take. You go quiet
when I tell you it'll grow into a frog
not a salamander, and when I explain in low tones
how it will do that, when I use the word *metamorphosis*
and claim you and I have followed
a similar path to now, you believe me in the tentative way
a seven-year-old believes a thing he doesn't understand
if the tone and the teller are true.
But a tadpole isn't what you want
to bridge us with today, so you let it go
and pick up where you left off
tilting rocks and looking under, lightly dredging
until you find one paddling

the mud that slipped
through your fingers and shriek as you run it
over boulders on rubber ankles
to the plastic container in my lap
where you pre-positioned water and a twig
to calm its robot legs and scratchy toes
that we might get a better look.
And when your mother suddenly crests
the ridge above us, calling out our names
in a voice foreshadowing what she found
when she bounds toward us over spongy red earth
you remember the dark she said
is in us all, gently let it go
and run uphill to get your fill
of the light behind her eyes
and hug her lumpy apron
full of chanterelles.

Better Things to Do

Because I was living in Oregon
I missed your funeral in Florida.

Decades passed. Wetlands became wetlands.
My watch pointed to whatever needed doing.
It was easy to fit forty years on the head of a pin.

And then I started driving
up buttes and down gullies, over calendars and lost photos
across silk scarves and ground limestone
until I found you, in Pompano, next to Grandma
where you'd been the whole time
two vaults above ground
like the one your father took back in Fossalto
a month before you sailed from there
to here.

Pompano was a good choice.
Blue and green, set back from the road
quiet and well-maintained.
But no *you* there, of course. No laugh
or whiff of red wine, no voice. Just two names
carved in Roman letters, resting side-by-side.

Orbiting the sun somewhere
drunk dancing with your father
you don't care it took me forty years to find you.

You've had better things to do
than worry if your chiseled name
became an asterisk.

Visiting my Great-Aunt's Grave, Kenesaw Nebraska

I'm passing through, Ellen,
on the way to the rest of my life.
It's been 90 years since you died. Even so, the fields are still
in alfalfa. Water still pushes up in a crescent of springs, clean
as air. Same stars, same moon. Not much has changed in
Kenesaw, population 932, where you cursed and laughed and
sweated and froze through the second half of your hundred-
year life. The same shimmering barns, same extra sun, the
same dusty roads plumbed with gravity. But the schoolhouse
you taught in is gone, and your garden and cow.

I've come to bring you flowers, Ellen, update you, run my
finger along your collar bone and straighten your long white
braid. You'd be surprised how much I know. I've read your
longhand, seen all the photos. I know you were an abolitionist,
a suffragist crank, a newspaper junkie, a prohibitionist, a
genealogist, an educator and a person of some letters. But
I imagine you too a free-thinker, a skeptic under stars, a
gender-nonconformist polished by winds that poured over the
Rockies, crossed the plains and found you standing in your
garden, leaning on a hoe.

It took me four days to drive here from Portland. I passed
through ancient forests, moonscapes and urban sprawl,
over plateaus bathed in celestial milk, past oxbows and
meanders, canyons, rock-faces and escarpments, each place
superimposed by a faded photo of you in a rocking chair with
a blanket in your lap and a cat in your arms.

Ellen, the topsoil on the hem of your long dress is lost. And
the two-room house you built with your teacher's salary. But
there's a gas station now, a brick school with a flagpole. The old
bank is a take-out deli.

I park on Main Street, stretch my legs and walk around. So this is where you stood up and shouted down your congressman at the Blue Bird Café. Where you sucker-punched your senator in the local paper. Where you wrote the brick-and-mortar history of our family, page-by-researched-page, until the old ones' chests, as you said, rose and fell again.

She and her sister's family were the first ones here, I tell the lady at City Hall, who doesn't know anyone in town with our last name. But she wouldn't. You never married, never had kids and your sister took the name Williams. But Ellen, I'll be your grandson from now on, if you'll let me. I'll keep your papers dry and feed your stray cat.

At the cemetery, a mile outside town, your stone is easy to find with its chiseled lyric and Yankee rationale:
Ellen Dorcas Harn
Born 1829, Frederick Maryland
Died 1930, Kenesaw Nebraska
101 years, 3 months, 12 days
40 years a teacher, 80 years a worker
for full citizenship for women.

Ellen, did someone put something tender in your casket? Like a folded poem, a woven jute bracelet or a beet-red rose? Did someone cut a lock of your hair and keep it to the end of their forever? Someone who's here too? Are the bones of your beloved here too?

Sitting cross-legged against a tree, facing your stone, eating my traveler's lunch, I say out loud everything I know about you. Your research, your teaching, your travels horse and rail. Your windmill, pine house and iron stove. Your speeches, op-eds and sign-held pickets. Your broken chimney and moonlit roof.

I say the story of your flight in a biplane, 90 years old in 1919,
the year the vote was won, unfurling a *Votes for Women* banner
over the rooftops and haystacks of Kenesaw below.

I say your brother's name, George, killed at Vicksburg, because
George was mine too. I say the name of your grandfather,
Caleb, who hid candy in his shirt pocket for you, because
Caleb was mine too. And I say that line from your niece's
poem that you saved for us when she drowned near here,
because Ellen, I'm a poet too.

I'm here, Ellen, because you wanted me to come
you left a trail
we are kin
and I was passing through.

In Dayton Ohio, in 1919,

Paul married a stenographer,
a girl from church with ice-blue eyes and sandy hair,
braided in the modern way. He was nineteen, assembling
pumps for Barney & Smith, the giant rail-car maker. They
talked about things over tea. Big things in quiet voices. Marie's
shy smile found his thin moustache. They loved the idea of
in-laws and children chattering inside a Catholic parentheses.
They were old enough, they said, to marry, and over time,
they were sure, they'd find the key had been left in heaven's
door. Marie was nowhere near pregnant when she stood at
the altar and Paul showed up with a briefcase in one hand
and a toolbox in the other, ready to join her little family of
women: Marie, her handicapped sister and a widowed mother
with deep-tissue memory of orphanage nuns. He didn't mind
crossing that threshold. It didn't faze him, the only man in
their tiny, rented house. He had what they lacked, knew who
they didn't. Every day, he took the trolley to his new job
downtown, bookkeeper for Lowe Brothers' Paint. Paul was
good with numbers. Marie watered hydrangeas with a tin can.
She perfected the timing of roast pork, sauerkraut, lemon
merengue pie and coffee. She learned the ballet of him opening
doors. Before long, they rented a house of their own, then
bought one, then another for Sister and Mom. And they raised
a son together, under a portrait of the Risen Savior hanging in
the hall. There was baseball in Dayton, competitive bowling,
and cutting-edge bunting left over from the Wright Brothers'
parade. Prosperity knocked down walls and unlatched latches.
It was easy to slip their only boy into the orbit of Jesus,
umbrella him against the Depression, follow him through
D-Day, law school, marriage and four grandsons. It just took
time. Marie cleaned her counters with lemon juice. Paul
repainted the living room. They expected change as they grew
older, but never Sherman tanks in the streets of Detroit, slick

grass at Kent State, a grandson in Saigon with a drip in one
arm and a needle in the other. Talking wore them out, twenty
words instead of one. TV took its place. They saw it as a sign
when Lawrence Welk looked pasty next to Neil and Buzz. And
when the angels finally came, to award them their pensions,
they were ready to go, worried if they stayed much longer, their
accounts might somehow expire. Paul went first. Then their
boy. Then Marie upon finding herself back where she started.
And their grandsons, dazed and unglued, filled-in for them as
best they could, as long as they could, then scattered,
tasked as they were but never given
maps, ropes or tools.

Death in the Age of Facebook
for Danny, 1952-2017

someone says you're with god now
someone is sorry as shit
someone lights a candle for you
someone freaks-out about mortality
someone says it was a privilege
someone posts a string of crying yellow faces
someone remembers seeing Cream with you at Cobo Hall
someone admires your compassion for downtrodden strangers
someone sees your face in the next full moon
someone sends their sincerest condolences
someone posts a video of you gulping vodka
someone calls you a mischievous saint
someone says you're surfing an astral plane now
someone shares a link to a John Prine song you loved
someone offers to help with the arrangements
someone *loves* everyone who's hurting
someone says they have no words
someone has no words
someone wails like a burning violin
someone calls you *Wild Man Harn*
someone will never forget
someone says *R.I.P.*
someone says *No*
someone feels joy
remembering you

Planks It Borrowed from the Wind

Walking the old neighborhood
after forty years away,
looking for the house I grew up in
by memory, by heart.

It doesn't take long. I turn a corner
dust kicks up, a bird bolts into the blue
crabgrass snags my laces.

And then I see it, our old front door
smaller and darker than I remember
but ours, definitely, ours.

None of us came close to seeing back then
how busy it was
returning planks it borrowed from the wind.
Christmas lights distracted us for a while
and paint rolled over handprints
while the attic, where the truth was
most obvious and least seen
hid behind its pull-string
ladder out of view.

In high school I remember thinking
this town was so mundane.
Grandparents aging around the dinner table.
Giant oaks upholding their fiction in the park.

Now, that's the last word I'd use.

Acknowledgements

Chiron Review	*He meets an old friend for beers*
Cloudbank	*Opposites*
Comstock Review	*Morning Walk*
	Girlfriend
Meridian	*In Dayton Ohio, in 1919,*
Pandemic Puzzle Poems	*Memory for Abe*
Poetry East	*Office*
	How to Pay for Napalm
Punch Drunk	*My neighbor the recluse and I*
Red Rock Review	*Salvation Army Finds $5,000 Diamond Ring in Donation Kettle*
Right Hand Pointing	*To be Of a Place and Not Just From*
SALT	*Lifting the Veil*
	Hendricks Park
	Visiting my Great-Aunt's Grave, Kenesaw, Nebraska

Notes

Visiting my Great-Aunt's Grave, Kenesaw, Nebraska was a finalist in the 2018 Arts & Letters Unclassifiable Contest.

In Dayton Ohio, in 1919, dedicated to my grandparents, Paul Harn and Marie Gladwish, was a finalist in the 2020 Meridian Short Prose Contest and nominated by Meridian for Best of the Net in 2021.

Yes, I kept your high school graduation picture is dedicated to Jeanne Culbertson.

To be Of a Place and not Just From was started in Dru Watkins' haiku workshop and is dedicated to him.

Eugene, Oregon, 1980, The Year You Were Born is dedicated to my daughter Emily Clugston Harn.

Why You Left Italy at Fourteen was started in a workshop taught by the late Peter Sears and is dedicated to him.

Hunting the Elusive Columbia Gorge Salamander is dedicated to my grandson, Abraham Clugston.

About the Author

JOHN HARN was raised in Michigan and lived his adult life in Oregon. His first full-length collection, *Physics for Beginners*, won the 2017 Blue Light Book Award and was published that year in San Francisco. His second collection, *Witness* (Kelsay Books), appeared in 2019. Now retired, he worked with international students for three decades in the US and abroad as a teacher and administrator. He's taught poetry workshops at the University of Oregon, Pacific University and the Oregon State Penitentiary and was a Teaching Artist at The University of Texas Medical Branch in Galveston. He has exhibited poems in several art galleries in Oregon and currently hosts the Studio 7 Poetry Reading Series in Eugene. His poems have appeared in *Carolina Quarterly, Chicago Quarterly, Denver Quarterly, Hotel Amerika, Miramar, New Orleans Review, Northwest Review, Pleiades, Post Road, Prairie Schooner, South Carolina Review, Spillway* and other journals. Married to Etsuko Matsunaga, he is the father of three grown daughters.